Ulf Wakenius'
OSCAR**PETERSON**LICKS
FORJAZZ**GUITAR**

Learn the Jazz Concepts of a Master Improviser

ULF**WAKENIUS**

With Tim Pettingale

FUNDAMENTAL**CHANGES**

Ulf Wakenius' Oscar Peterson Licks for Jazz Guitar

Learn the Jazz Concepts of a Master Improviser

ISBN: 978-1-78933-216-2

Published by **www.fundamental-changes.com**

Copyright © 2020 Ulf Wakenius

www.fundamental-changes.com

Over 11,000 fans on Facebook: **FundamentalChangesInGuitar**

Instagram: **FundamentalChanges**

For over 350 Free Guitar Lessons with Videos Check Out

www.fundamental-changes.com

Cover Image Copyright: Rolf Ohlson, used with permission.

Acknowledgements

I want to extend my deepest thanks to my Canadian family, Kelly and Celine Peterson for giving me permission to do this project. Many thanks to Chris Parson and the Stratford Festival for permission to use the internal photos, and thanks to Rolf Ohlson for the cover photo. Thanks also to Tim, Joseph and Levi at Fundamental Changes, and to Martin Taylor for recommending me. Finally, thanks to Oscar Peterson for making my dreams come true.

–*Ulf Wakenius*

Contents

About the Author

Ulf Wakenius is an acclaimed Swedish jazz guitarist. Between 1997 and 2007 Ulf held one of the most prestigious spots in jazz for a guitar player: a chair in the Oscar Peterson Quartet. Prior to this, Ulf's career had already included many record breaking moments. His duo, Guitars Unlimited, performed at the culmination of the 1985 Melody Grand Prix, an event seen by over 600 million viewers. It was probably the largest audience a jazz guitar duo has ever had!

Shortly afterwards, Ulf began an extremely successful and long-lasting collaboration with the legendary Danish bass player Niels-Henning Örsted Pedersen. This was followed with two successful albums with bass icon Ray Brown, both of which topped the US Jazz Charts.

Ulf is known for his great rhythmic feel and lyrical touch, and many of the world's most influential jazz guitarist are amongst his fans:

"He plays the guitar like he was born with it already in his hands."

–John McLaughlin

"Just great!"

–Pat Metheny

"So you are the bad boy everybody's talking about?!"

–Larry Carlton

"Spectacular! Unbelievable!"

–Allan Holdsworth

"I heard you with Ray Brown, you sounded great!"

–John Scofield

"Humongous chops!"

–Pat Martino

For more information, visit: **ulfwakenius.net**

Introduction

In the mid-nineties I had the privilege of playing with the great Ray Brown's trio and we recorded two albums together in New York at CBS studios – *Seven Steps to Heaven* and *Summertime*. Ray had worked with Oscar Peterson for around fifteen years, and Oscar had huge respect for him, so naturally these recordings came to his attention. This was the first time I came onto Oscar's radar.

At the same time, Oscar's current bass player happened to be my close friend, Niels-Henning Ørsted Pedersen (NHOP) – another bass genius – and NHOP was aware that Oscar was looking for a new guitar player. He told Oscar that he knew a guy who would be perfect for him, so NHOP was instrumental in opening the door for me.

One day, Oscar's agent telephoned me out of the blue and asked if I'd consider joining the Oscar Peterson quartet. I was literally speechless. I managed to say, "Wow! Of course." Then he spoke about getting me to Munich for the first event that was booked in the diary. I asked him, "What music do I need to learn?" but all he said was, "Forget about the music, just bring your tuxedo!"

I was informed that my first gig with Oscar would be at the Munich Philharmonie and that I'd meet him on the day of the gig. I had no clue what I was going to play when I got there, but the gig was two months away, so I spent that time tracking down Oscar's many CDs and listening to his arrangements. It was fifteen years' worth of material – a lot of listening!

The day of the gig came and I was instructed to meet Oscar at a little rehearsal studio near the venue. I got set up and Oscar walked in, sat down at the piano and just began to play. I recognised the tune as *Here's That Rainy Day* and thought, "Great, I know that one" and joined in. After a while, Oscar stopped playing and said, "Sounds good. See you at the concert" and with that he left.

That was my "rehearsal". Then came the evening concert. We were literally about to step onto the stage when I nervously asked NHOP, "Well, what are we going to play tonight?!" All he said to me was, "We'll find out!" We began with a turnaround and I learnt that at each show, the band would come out and begin playing, one by one; first drums, then bass, then guitar, before Oscar came out. That night we played the turnaround until the full band was on stage, then Oscar launched into the well-known standard, *Falling in Love With Love*. "OK," I thought, "I'm going to be fine."

However, next Oscar began playing one of his original compositions – one which hadn't appeared during the vast amount of research I'd done. I knew I had to find the tonal centre of this tune very quickly. It didn't matter that I didn't know the melody, but pretty soon I was going to have to take a solo – and in front of 7,000 people. I knew I was just going to have to go for it. It was what I call a musical bungee jump!

That night I discovered that Oscar was a very spontaneous guy, and he liked to play whatever he felt in the moment. I've since told many guitar students, "There are some situations in music that you *cannot* prepare for – you just have to go with it."

At the end of the gig, I said to myself, "Look on the bright side, Ulf. You got to play with Oscar Peterson once in your lifetime. Now he's going to send you home!" But Oscar's wife called me into his dressing room and he told me, "Young man, you did great tonight. Consider yourself hired." That was the second moment of amazement for me.

It was the start of an incredible ten years together, during which time I was privileged to tour the world with Oscar. We became family during that time. I owe so much to Oscar and his legacy, it seems only fitting to dedicate this book to my dear friend and mentor. His legacy lives on.

Ulf Wakenius, July 2020.

(L-R: Ulf Wakenius, Niels-Henning Ørsted Pedersen, Oscar Peterson, Martin Drew)

About this Book

Oscar Emmanuel Peterson is widely regarded as one of the greatest jazz pianists of all time. He possessed all the attributes needed to make him the "complete" musician: effortless technique and dexterity, a swinging "in the pocket" sense of time, a vast vocabulary of melodic ideas, an in-depth understanding of hamony, and an energetic creativity that propelled his music forward.

As a child Oscar studied piano with renowned Hungarian-born pianist Paul de Marky, who had studied under Franz Liszt. This early training provided him with a strong Classical foundation – an influence he would carry throughout his career in jazz. At the same time as studying the Classical repertoire, he was enthralled by the exciting sound of Boogie Woogie piano and began to investigate that music.

Aged nine, Peterson would practice for up to six hours each day, and aged fourteen he won a national music competition. This led to him dropping out of High School in Montreal to pursue a professional music career. Peterson's career hit next level success when he was "discovered" by jazz impresario Norman Granz. Granz happened to hear Peterson while he was taking a cab to the airport, via a radio broadcast from a Montreal jazz club. He was so impressed that he told the cab driver to turn around and take him to the club. Granz would become Peterson's manager for most of his career.

Oscar's style

Oscar's Classical influence remained a thread in his playing, and jazz journalists commented that at times his ballad playing was reminiscent of Ravel or Debussy. Equally, the blues was never far from his melodic improvisations. One of his great inspirations was Art Tatum, and Peterson exhibited the same kind of unbridalled virtuosity. Oscar's left hand was a strong as his right, which meant he could play lightening speed runs, mirrored in both hands. His focus on technical prowess sometimes irritated the music critics, but it was praised by those whose opinions mattered most. Duke Ellington called him "the Maharaja of the keyboard" and said that Peterson was "beyond category", while legendary pianist Hank Jones said he was "head and shoulders above any pianist alive today."

Benny Green commented about Art Tatum that he was the only jazz musician to "attempt to conceive a style based on *all styles*, to master the mannerisms of the schools, then synthesize those into something personal." But Peterson achieved the same feat as his hero, harmonizing all of his influences into a cohesive whole.

Oscar's influence on jazz guitar

It's clear that Oscar enjoyed working with guitar players. When Ulf Wakenius joined the Oscar Peterson Quartet in 1997 (a tenure that would last a decade), he was preceded by Barney Kessel, Herb Ellis and Joe Pass. It's not overstating the case to say that Oscar's playing seeped into the conscious of the jazz guitar community though his influence on these four great players.

Oscar publicly referred to Ulf as "one of the greatest guitar players alive in the world today" and Ulf is uniquely placed to write this book, which shows how Oscar's mastery of jazz on piano can be adapted onto the guitar.

So, what can guitar players learn from Oscar Peterson?

Oscar's playing demonstrates a deep understanding of harmony and he would often reharmonize well-known tunes in a beautiful way that brought something fresh, while preserving the original intention of the composer.

His solos feature chord solos and octave patterns, coupled with bluesy double-stops. He retained a Liszt-like approach to playing melodies, taking a simple melodic motif and developing endless variations of it. He was also a master of bebop phrasing and soloing, and used bebop techniques such as enclosures, chromaticism and substitution ideas. Oscar's improvised single-line runs were so beautifully formed and richly harmonic that a better question is, what *can't* we learn from Oscar Peterson!

In this book, each chapter is dedicated to an aspect of Oscar's technique and Ulf expertly demonstrates how these concepts transfer onto guitar. As well as gaining an insight into all the techniques of modern jazz guitar, you'll discover a resource that will add to your jazz vocabulary for years to come.

As Oscar said himself, "It doesn't matter what the instrument is, it's simply another means of expression."

Tim Pettingale

Get the Audio

The audio files for this book are available to download for free from **www.fundamental-changes.com.** The link is in the top right-hand corner. Click on the "Guitar" link then simply select this book title from the drop-down menu and follow the instructions to get the audio.

We recommend that you download the files directly to your computer, not to your tablet, and extract them there before adding them to your media library. You can then put them onto your tablet, iPod or burn them to CD. On the download page there are instructions and we also provide technical support via the contact form.

For over 350 free guitar lessons with videos check out:

www.fundamental-changes.com

Over 11,000 fans on Facebook: **FundamentalChangesInGuitar**

Tag us for a share on Instagram: **FundamentalChanges**

Chapter One – The Blues

"I play as I feel."

–O.P.

The blues was never far from Oscar's playing and all of the devices one would expect to hear in a blues player's vocabulary are present in his solos, such as:

- Licks with a bluesy inflection, played behind the beat

- Pentatonic single line runs

- Attacking double-stops and octave lines

In this chapter, you'll learn some jazz-blues licks to add to your vocabulary using each of these techniques.

The origins of jazz are in the blues so it's vital for any jazz guitarist to have an understanding of the blues and how it informs the style of modern jazz we know today.

The blues is soulful, visceral music that connects on an emotional level so it's important to have some blues licks in your melodic arsenal. But you don't want to just throw the occasional bluesy lick into your playing, you want to weave blues lines into the narrative of your solo and this is something Oscar did very naturally. In jazz guitar circles, Kenny Burrell managed to retain a very bluesy element to his playing, but did so in a seamless way, smoothly switching between blues phrases and bebop lines.

Technique tips

- Don't underestimate the usefulness of the minor pentatonic scale in jazz. Make sure you know your pentatonic scales inside out and using the range of the neck, not just in the well-known box positions

- Listen to some of the blues greats like B.B. King. The masters can take a simple phrase, pack it with emotion and get lots of mileage out of it. Also listen to those players who cross over from blues into jazz, like Larry Carlton and Robben Ford.

In Example 1a, I play a stock blues phrase over a jazz blues progression in Bb Major. It's a simple line, but notice how I repeat the phrase, keeping it the same even when the chords change underneath. The line works equally well over the I chord (Bb7), the IV chord (Eb9) and the V chord (F9).

Example 1a

Here's another example of how you can incorporate a standard blues phrase into a jazz blues. This one is played in octaves over an F blues.

Example 1b

Example 1c uses a jazzier line, but sticks to the technique of looping the phrase. I won't show all the bars of the progression this time, but the line still works over every chord in the progression and you can hear it played in full in the audio example. The three-note pickup phrase is only played once, at the beginning.

Example 1c

Oscar was well known for playing lines in octaves (we'll explore this more in Chapter Four) and it's a technique that transfers easily onto guitar. Here is a bluesy Bb riff played in octaves. Use plenty of attack, and adjust the position of your fretting hand so that you mute the middle string between the octave notes. Again, it works over the entire blues sequence, as you'll hear in the audio.

Example 1d

Here is another simple pentatonic line to play over a Bb blues where rhythmic variation in the key to making it work. One easy way to increase your jazz vocabulary is to take a lick you know and vary it rhythmically, for example, by starting it on different beats of the bar. If you often play a particular lick on beat 1 of the bar, listen to how it sounds when played on beat 3, crossing the bar line into the next measure.

Example 1e

Here's an idea that relies on space and rhythm.

Example 1f

Now try this pentatonic lick that features a straight run down the blues scale. Repeating it over the changing chord sequence is what makes it interesting.

Example 1g

Example 1h is a slightly more complicated pentatonic-blues motif idea that contains bigger interval jumps.

Example 1h

Jazz pianists often slur notes to play bluesy phrases, hitting more than one note at once and effectively "sliding" from one note to the next. On guitar, we play these ideas as double-stops. Unlike a conventional double-stop, however, the aim is to hit the first note cleanly, then slide into the next note a fraction later. This is especially important in bar 10, where the slightly lazy and "imprecise" way of playing the phrase captures the pianistic sliding feel.

Listen to the audio to get the idea.

Example 1i

Example 1j is a riff-like motif that places a slurred double-stop into a common blues phrase. There is a quite a bit of space in this lick and once again it's all about the rhythmic phrasing. Play it a few times to make sure it's really sounding in the pocket.

Example 1j

Lastly, Example 1k features a favourite Oscar lick that adapts nicely onto guitar. It's a double-stop where one note is held as a pedal tone while other notes ascend against it. Unlike some of the licks we've looked at, this lick is transposed when the chord changes, instead of staying the same.

Play this using all downstrokes and don't dampen the notes so they ring against each other.

Example 1k

In the next chapter we'll explore the vocal phrasing aspect of Oscar's jazz-blues.

Chapter Two – Vocal Phrasing

"If you have something to say of any worth, then people will listen to you."

Oscar's own words say it best. How do we play so that people will listen? It's easy to grab people's attention with flashy guitar licks and technique, but to really *connect* on an emotional level, a soulful, lyrical approach achieves so much more. The solos that people tend to remember are those that have strong melodies and vocal-like phrasing to the lines. No one leaves a gig humming the Symmetrical Diminished scale!

How can we achieve this vocal quality in our playing?

We can learn from several musical devices that Oscar loved to use. In essence, it all comes down to good phrasing. Just as a long sentence with no punctuation is hard to process and understand, so a solo with poor phrasing will lack structure and direction. When we play well-composed phrases, however, our solos begin to tell a story and it is this storytelling that audiences relate to.

To develop this approach, listen to some of the great jazz singers and hear how they form melodies and improvise scat-phrases. For a great example, check out Carmen McRae's version of *Satin Doll* on the album *The Great American Songbook*. It's a lesson in superb phrasing (and it also contains a burning solo by Joe Pass!)

Once again, the blues helps us to achieve this vocal quality in our jazz guitar lines and can be broken down into several techniques that easily give your lines vocal phrasing:

- Call and response

- Taking a breath

- Rhythmic variation

- Making lines swing

We'll explore each one in turn.

Technique tips

- To develop the concepts in this chapter, transcribe some great jazz singers performing a tune that you know. Transcribing a vocalist will teach you a lot about good phrasing

- Sing your phrases as you play so that you are forced to take a musical "breath" between lines. If this technique is new to you, sing a single line to begin with, then work out how to play it on the guitar. This will help with your ear training. The ultimate aim is to be able to think of a line, then sing and play it simultaneously. It doesn't matter if you're no great singer – just sing quietly!

Call and response

The first technique we'll look at is "call and response", which means to play one melodic statement followed by another answering phrase with a breath in between. The first statement might be a very simple phrase before the second echoes it with a variation.

Sometimes you'll hear the first statement repeated several times with the "response" varying each time, which creates an easy way to tell a story.

Here are some call and response licks to get you started.

Example 2a

In the blues, it's common to mix major and minor licks over a dominant chord, and in Example 2b the line spells out a Bbm6 arpeggio over the Bb7 chord.

Example 2b

Notice that even if you don't want to play the notes of a call and response phrase the same way each time, mimicking its rhythm can just as effective. This is the idea behind Example 2c.

Example 2c

So far, the call and response lines have been very bluesy. Here's a jazzier version.

Example 2d

Taking a breath

In jazz, where virtuosity is applauded, it can take great self-discipline to leave space in our phrasing. However, the notes we leave out are just as important as the ones we put in. Never be afraid of leaving space. In Example 2e I deliberately leave a *very* big breath to emphasise this – two whole bars in fact! But this pause makes the lick stand out all the more.

Example 2e

Here's a call and response lick that contains a short two-note phrase at the beginning, but leaves significant breathing space before giving the response. It works because it adds an element of surprise.

Example 2f

Rhythmic variation

A simple line that has a strong rhythmic feel will always be more memorable than one played with little or no inflection. Example 2g is a line with chromatic notes that *pulls* against the beat and its insistent repeating rhythm grabs the listener's attention.

Example 2g

Example 2h is a line using standard bebop vocabulary in the style of Joe Pass. We will explore chromatic passing notes more in a later chapter, but essentially the phrase outlines the chord tones of the underlying chord and approaches them from a half step below.

This outside note/inside note approach gives the listener enough information about the harmony, but keeps things interesting with the chromatics. Listen to the audio and practice the lick until you know it well enough to play it with a strong rhythmic feel.

Example 2h

Making lines swing

One of the key skills a jazz musician learns over time is how to make their lines swing. The element of *swing* is notoriously difficult to convey using notation (or even words!). Instead it has to be heard, and absorbed into your consciousness over time.

Swing relies on having such a strong internal sense of time that you are able to *play around* with it, placing some notes in front of the beat, some dead on the beat, and some behind. When jazz soloists swing, they play in front *and* behind the beat to create a *push-pull* effect, while never losing sight of the "centre" of the beat.

Guitar players have a tendency to rush (we are eager like that!), but jazz demands a more laid-back approach. To practice swing, play with a metronome and initially focus only on playing a little behind the beat. Exaggerate this to begin with – even to the point where you feel you are too far behind. Leave some space between your phrases. Now try recording yourself and listen back. Often when we think we are playing with too much of a lazy feel, we're actually spot on. Sustained practice with a metronome will help you to nail the right feel. Also play along to some good quality backing tracks.

In Example 2j I play the first phrase slightly in front of the beat, which gives it an urgency, but then I pull things back with a behind-the-beat bluesy phrase. The hammer-on/pull-off phrase in bars four and eight helps with the *pull* effect.

Example 2i

Another vocal-phrasing technique that helps things to swing is to "pop out" certain notes in a phrase, just as a singer might emphasise certain words or phrases.

Example 2j

Lastly, here is a Charlie Christian-inspired line that combines a swing feel with rhythmic variation, and also includes breathing spaces. There are plenty of great jazz standard backing tracks on YouTube, so pick one of your favourite tunes to play along to and practice all the elements of phrasing we've covered here.

Example 2k

Chapter Three – Developing Motifs

"I don't think you should speak until you have your sentence together in your mind. It's easier to listen to someone who knows what he wants to say than a person who stops, starts, picks up another idea, continues, and winds up with a series of chopped-up phrases."

One characteristic of Oscar's Classical training that he maintained throughout his playing career was *ostinato* technique. *Ostinato* is a compositional technique that originated in the Baroque period of Classical music. It describes a phrase or motif in a piece of music that persistently repeats (the literal English translation of the Italian word is "obstinate").

An ostinato can be based around repeating rhythms, repeating notes, or even repeating an entire melodic phrase. In its strictest "Classical" sense, an ostinato phrase is identical each time, but it has come to encompass variations and the development of motifs. This idea has found its way into modern jazz and also pop music (The Verve's *Bitter Sweet Symphony* is a perfect example of its use). In jazz, it's often referred to simply as a *motif*, and is often varied to fit the chord changes.

Technique tips

- Listen to some of Jim Hall's recordings. The idea of taking a motif and developing it throughout a tune is a key element of his playing. Also check out Julian Lage for a more complex take on the technique.

- Play slowly through the changes of one of your favourite tunes. Play a simple phrase, then explore what needs to change about the phrase to make it work over the next chord. Sometimes you won't need to change anything at all, and other times changing just one note can make it fit. See how far you can push this idea.

Developing simple motifs

The first three examples show how to develop a simple motif, then carry it through a set of changes. These ideas are based on the changes of the tune *You Look Good to Me*.

In Example 3a, a phrase is stated that spans bars one and two. In bars three and four, this phrase is mimicked rhythmically, but the notes are adapted to fit the chord change. In bar five, a new idea appears – a simple four-note motif. This motif is repeated and adapted slightly to accommodate the changes. To provide a contrast, I play a bluesy line to finish.

Example 3a

Next, here is a longer example that can serve as a study piece for your practice sessions. It should give you a clear idea of how to take one phrase and develop it across a set of chord changes with minimal alteration. To prevent this idea from becoming repetitive I play a different type of line that includes approach notes in bars 13-16, before returning to the motif idea.

Example 3b

Example 3c shows how this approach can be incorporated as part of a solo. The motif is slightly more complex here and it doesn't run all the way through the solo, so the effect is more subtle than in the licks we've seen so far. However, listen to the entire solo and you can hear how each idea is developed.

Example 3c

The next example takes an ostinato approach to developing a motif. The main "question" phrase is played the same each time but the response is always different. A simple idea like this can give your solos a strong sense of narrative and direction as it gives the listener something concrete to hold onto. The lines that surround the ostinato can be as wild as you like!

Example 3d

Pedal tone ideas

A pedal tone is a device used to create tension and release in jazz and can be used both melodically and harmonically. Melodically, we can play phrases that contain a repeating note, while other notes around it change. Harmonically, we might play the same chord for several bars before returning to the proper chord progression.

Typically this works best by pedalling the V7 chord. So, for instance, in a Rhythm Changes tune, instead of playing the normal I vi ii V eight-bar sequence (Bbmaj7 – G7 – Cm7 – F7, etc), we can play eight bars of F11. The F11 chord wants to resolve to the tonal centre of Bb Major, but we ratchet up the tension by making it last much longer.

Example 3e combines both of these ideas with a repeating riff over a pedal tone chord.

Example 3e

Example 3f also combines melodic and harmonic pedal tones. This is not the kind of device we can use all the time, but when used sparingly it can be extremely effective. Notice that this lick also has a bit of a classical feel.

Example 3f

Oscar's classical influence

Oscar would sometimes play motif variations just like a Classical pianist but over jazz chords. He tended to play these lines quite straight, without swinging too hard, and they contained very few passing notes to create an effect like a Classical etude.

Example 3g

Here's a variation of the previous idea that uses a cascading descending line. Play this line straight and unaccompanied and you'll immediately hear the Classical influence. Add a slight swing feel and some jazz chords, however, and it suddenly morphs into an exciting jazzy motif.

Example 3h

Finally, here's a longer study piece to study in your practice sessions. The motif idea is to simply take a four-note phrase and carry it through the chord progression. The rhythm of the four notes is the glue that holds everything together. In the final five bars I break away from the motif and use some blues vocabulary.

In this example I used a few *enclosures* (chromatic approaches to chord tones). Don't worry about these for now – we'll study them in detail in Chapter Six.

Example 3i

Chapter Four – Soloing With Chord Phrases

"I believe in using the entire piano as a single instrument, capable of expressing every possible musical idea."

In order to bring color and variety to his playing, Oscar would often break from using single line runs and play melodic phrases using block chords or octaves. These are pianistic ideas that jazz guitarists have been quick to absorb, and both techniques hinge on the idea of augmenting a melodic line.

With octaves, there is a simple doubling of the melody. The way that octaves are laid out on guitar serves to thicken the sound and allows us to play with more attack. Wes Montgomery is the master of octave use and you'll hear him play some quite complex lines with this technique.

Using block chords to solo is essentially the same concept – we have a melodic line and we want to augment it. This time, however, the approach is to build a small chord voicing on each note of the melody. Instead of a counter-*melody*, block chord soloing is like playing a counter-*harmony*.

This technique is a test of both our harmonic vocabulary and our ability to visualize chord voicings all over the fretboard. Again, Wes Montgomery took this idea and developed it beautifully. If you listen to Wes solo, you'll notice that he frequently plays a chorus of single line phrases, then moves to octaves, and ends with block chord soloing. Johnny Smith was also a master of this technique and often used lush sounding chord voicings in his solos.

Octave Technique tips

- Be sure to listen to some Wes Montgomery solos – essential for both chord soloing and octave ideas!

- Both Wes and George Benson make extensive use of octaves in their solos. When playing octave lines, adjust your fretting hand position so that you mute the string in between the octave notes – we don't want that to sound at all. Hit the octave with plenty of attack in your picking hand as it's important to make the notes sound as closely in unison as possible. George and Wes both tend to use their thumb for octaves to achieve a warmer sound, but it's fine to use a pick.

Let's explore some octave-based lines and begin with a classic Wes-style lick that spans the blues sequence with a slight modification to accommodate the Eb7 chord.

Example 4a

Here's a simple octave lick based around the major pentatonic scale. Though it's not hard to play, the strong rhythm makes this line memorable. In the audio, you'll hear that this two-bar phrase can be played over the entire blues sequence without modification.

Example 4b

Here's another octave lick that works for a blues progression. In bars 9-10 I break up the pattern with a syncopated line.

Example 4c

Here is a question and answer style line that's reminiscent of the great Kenny Burrell. This four-bar phrase can be looped and in the audio you'll hear it played over the full blues sequence.

Example 4d

Next, here's a Wes-inspired lick that descends chromatically.

Example 4e

Here's a final octave idea. The restriction which octave playing places on us (we can't physically play lots of notes), forces us to play stronger rhythmic ideas, so it's a good technique to create memorable hooks.

Example 4f

Now let's study some examples of block chord playing in solos.

Oscar would sometimes play block chords with *extended* voicings that are easier to achieve on the piano with its linear layout. On guitar, it's normal to use stripped down four-note voicings to create the block chord sound.

Example 4g is a study piece that demonstrates how to solo with block chords over a G Major blues progression. (These are the exact changes used on the Milt Jackson tune *Bags' Groove*, which was a favorite of Wes Montgomery's).

Listen to the audio for this example, then slowly play through the notation. Once you've heard the piece and played it, I'll give an overview of the techniques used to create this example.

Example 4g

On the face of it, this is a complex example with a lot of moving parts, but it's easier to understand if we break things down into the three principles on which nearly all block chord solos are built. Each principle describes a technique that you can work to develop during your practice times.

Principle 1: Use multiple voicings for chords

Look at bar two. The notated chord is C7 and there are four different chord voicings that broadly describe the C dominant sound. In order, we have C6 (played twice), C7b9 played in eighth position, C7b9 in eleventh position, and CMaj9(13).

If you want to develop the art of block chord soloing, the most important first step is to work out multiple voicings for chords across the range of the neck. Fundamental Changes have several resources that can help with this. Check out Joseph Alexander's *Jazz Guitar Chord Mastery*, and Tim Pettingale's *Jazz Guitar Chord Creativity*. They contain easy-to-follow systems that will increase your chord vocabulary and get you playing chord voicings all over the fretboard.

Principle 2: Use the versatile diminished chord shape

You'll recognise the first chord in bar one as a common diminished chord shape. This crops up a lot in block chord solos and is useful for two reasons:

First, it's a *multipurpose shape*. The chord played in twelfth position here could be interpreted as F diminished (with the F root on the high E string). But if we add a G bass note, it creates a G7b9 sound. The fourth chord in bar one, played in ninth position could be read as D diminished, but again, with a G bass note it becomes G7b9. The beauty of this little shape is that it's very easy to move around, and the context in which it's used determines how our ears perceive it.

Second, it's super-useful as a *connecting chord*. Look at bar one again. The diminished shape is used to chromatically connect the two voicings of G7b9. In jazz, you'll often see diminished or half-diminished chords used as approach/connecting chords. For instance, the progression Cmaj7 – Dm7 – Em7, can be played: Cmaj7 – C#dim – Dm7 – Ebm7b5 – Em7.

You can use diminished chords in block soloing the same way that you'd use non-scale tones as approach notes in single-line phrases. They work well because they want to resolve to the next chord in the sequence.

Principle 3: Make movements in minor thirds

Take another look at bar one. It contains another useful device for constructing block chord solos: movements in minor thirds (a distance of three frets on guitar). The first chord in the sequence is G7b9 in twelfth position, and the fourth chord is G7b9 in ninth position – a distance of a minor third. It's very common in jazz to shift things up or down in minor thirds, and this works for both chord cadences and licks.

Check out bar nine too. The notated chord is Am7. I'm aiming to play an Am9 chord here, but we don't hear the Am9 until the last beat of the bar. First, I ascend chromatically to a Cm9 in eighth position, then descend chromatically to the Am9. It's the minor third shift at work (Cm9 to Am9) and its purpose is to create a moment of tension and resolution.

Bearing these principles in mind, here's an alternative way of playing block chord phrases on this progression.

Example 4h

You may be saying to yourself at this point, "That's great, Ulf, but how can I come up with phrases like this myself?" Here's a useful tip:

First compose a simple, single-line melodic phrase over a chord progression using only notes located on the high E and B strings. Now try to harmonise that line into four-note block chords. If you need some help, there are online tools such as **https://oolimo.com/guitarchords/analyze** where you can move notes about on a virtual fretboard until you find a pleasing voicing.

Work with the original phrase you played until you come up with a set of small voicings that sound good together – and don't forget to use a diminished chord to connect the notes if you need to.

Here are some short examples of how to do this (there is no audio for these exercises).

First, here is a simple three note melody in the key of C Major.

There are many ways in which we can turn these single notes into block chord phrases. Here's one:

Equally, we could harmonise it this way. Here I make use of the half diminished shape and decide to make the final chord an Fmaj9, rather than Cmaj7.

Or we could create a more tense sound by harmonising the line with extended/altered chords.

Cmaj7   C#maj7(#11)   E7#9

The only limit to harmonising lines is your fretboard knowledge and imagination, so why not compose some melodic lines and see how many different ways you can harmonise them?

Example 4i is a line that mixes octave riffs with block chord phrases. This example shows how you can introduce block chords to punctuate a lick – a bit like comping for yourself while soloing.

Example 4i

In the next chapter we'll take the idea of chord soloing a step further and I'll demonstrate how to chord-solo over some famous standard tunes.

Chapter Five – Reharmonization Ideas

"I don't do something because I think it will sell 30 million albums. I couldn't care less. If it sells one, it sells one."

The ideas in this chapter take the concept of block chord soloing a little further, and build on the concepts discussed in the previous chapter. Here you'll find some examples that demonstrate how to harmonise melodic lines that are played over the chord changes to some famous jazz standards.

One ability of Oscar's that I admired greatly was his gift of being able to take a well-known tune and *reharmonize* it. In other words, he would enrich the existing harmony by adding extended chords, but also introduce chord substitution ideas. He could breath new life into an old tune, and yet never lose sight of the essence of the original harmony. Oscar would spend hours at the piano each day practicing chord voicings, forcing himself to be creative and trying different approaches. He once said, "I didn't want to sound like I played a chord just to get to the next one."

The concept of reharmonization is a big one and we can barely scratch the surface within the constraints of this book. However, I wanted to include this chapter because it was an important part of Oscar's style and because I hope it will inspire you to explore this concept further.

All the great jazz guitarists have included rehamonization ideas in their playing to produce wonderful chord-based solos. Joe Pass and my dear friend Martin Taylor are both examples of players who are *harmonic improvisers.* In other words, they come up with endless variations for the harmony of a tune and may never play it the same way twice.

In this chapter I want to give you two block chord solo ideas for you to work on before we end the chapter with an improvised solo guitar arrangement I played that weaves together single-note lines with chordal passages. The aim of this is to demonstrate to you how these ideas can eventually combine to create an original arrangement of a tune.

The first tune is the classic *Secret Love*, famously sung by Doris Day in the movie *Calamity Jane*.

Secret Love

We'll be looking at the A section of this tune. Here is the original A section chord sequence:

| Ebmaj7 Bb7 | Ebmaj7 Bb7 | Eb7 Ab7 Gm7 C7 | Fm7 Bb7 |

| Fm7 Bb7 | Fm7 Bb7 | Fm7 Bb7 | Eb6 Bb7 |

Example 5a is a block chord solo based on these changes. Remember, most of the time a block chord solo will be based on a single-note melody that has been harmonised into chords. If you play *only* the highest note on each chord shape below, you'll hear the counter-melody I had in mind when playing this tune.

Take your time playing through this. Compare it to the original changes and you'll see that most of the time I am using more complex sounding voicings, and adding passing chords to connect the *main* chords of the piece.

Example 5a

Satin Doll

Satin Doll was composed by Duke Ellington and Billy Strayhorn and is one of the all-time great jazz standards because it has a very memorable melodic hook, and includes a couple of simple, but highly effective harmonic twists. Here are the original A section changes:

| Cm7 F7 | Cm7 F7 | Dm7 G7 | Dm7 G7 |

| Gm7 C7 | Gbm7 B7 | Bbma7 Eb7 | Dm7 G7 |

Now here is my take on a chord solo. I'm using some b5 substitutions here to create extra movement.

Example 5b

Yours Is My Heart Alone

Finally, here's a study piece you can work on during your practice sessions which I improvised in free time. It's based on the changes to the song *Yours Is My Heart Alone*. This piece originated as an aria from the 1929 German operetta *Das Land des Lächelns* (The Land of Smile) with music written by Franz Lehár. During the 1940s it found its way out of the operatic arena and into jazz when Glenn Miller and Bing Crosby both recorded versions.

I deliberately threw the kitchen sink at this arrangement in terms of the harmonic structure, but don't be put off! Study a couple of bars at a time and first memorise the top line melody (the highest note of each chord) to give you a clear idea of where the melody line is heading. Some of the chordal harmonies are challenging but they all work together in context to create a pleasing arrangement. Listen to the audio a few times before you begin.

Example 5c

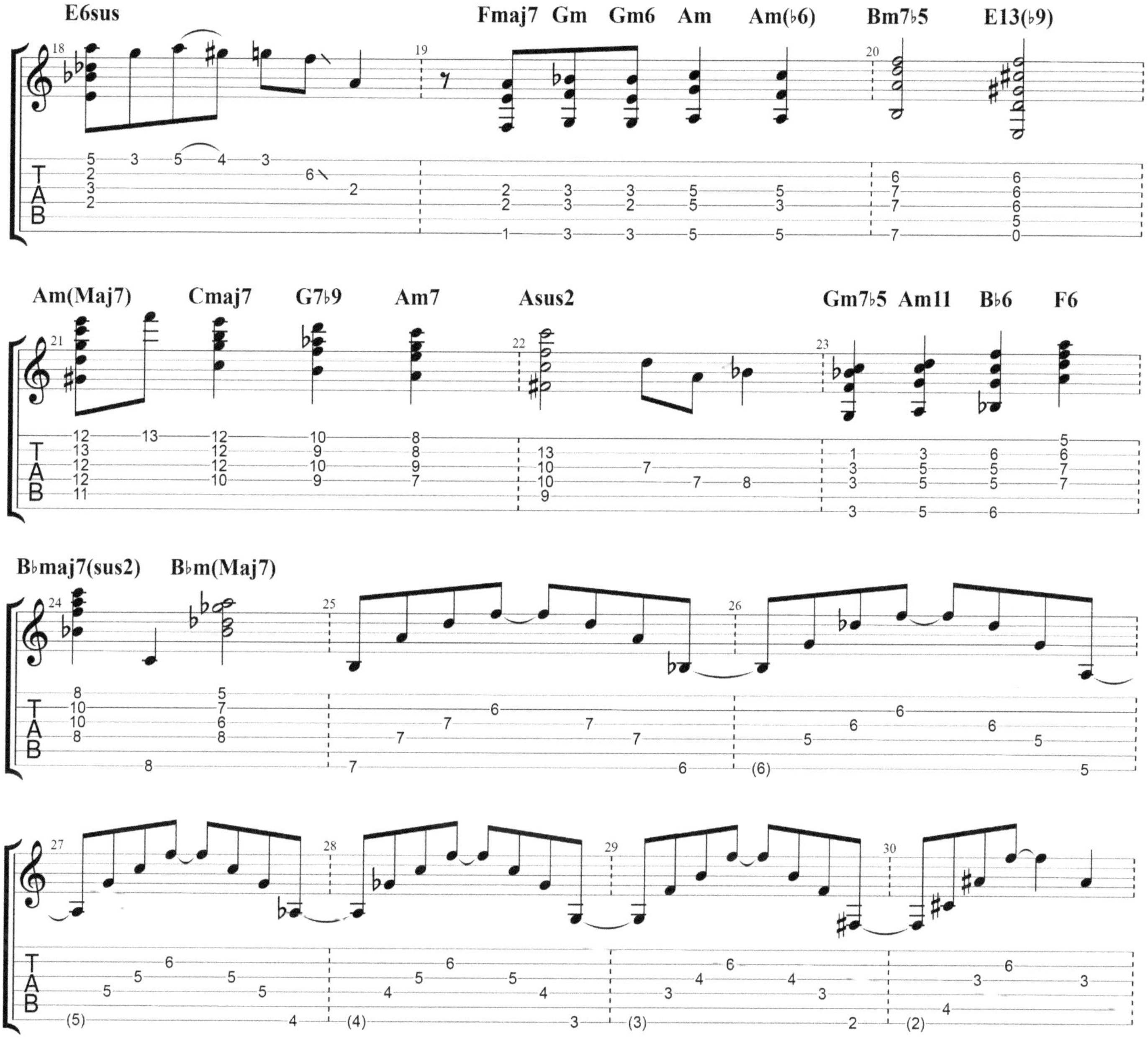
E6sus
Fmaj7
Gm
Gm6
Am
Am(♭6)
Bm7♭5
E13(♭9)
Am(Maj7)
Cmaj7
G7♭9
Am7
Asus2
Gm7♭5
Am11
B♭6
F6
B♭maj7(sus2)
B♭m(Maj7)
TAB

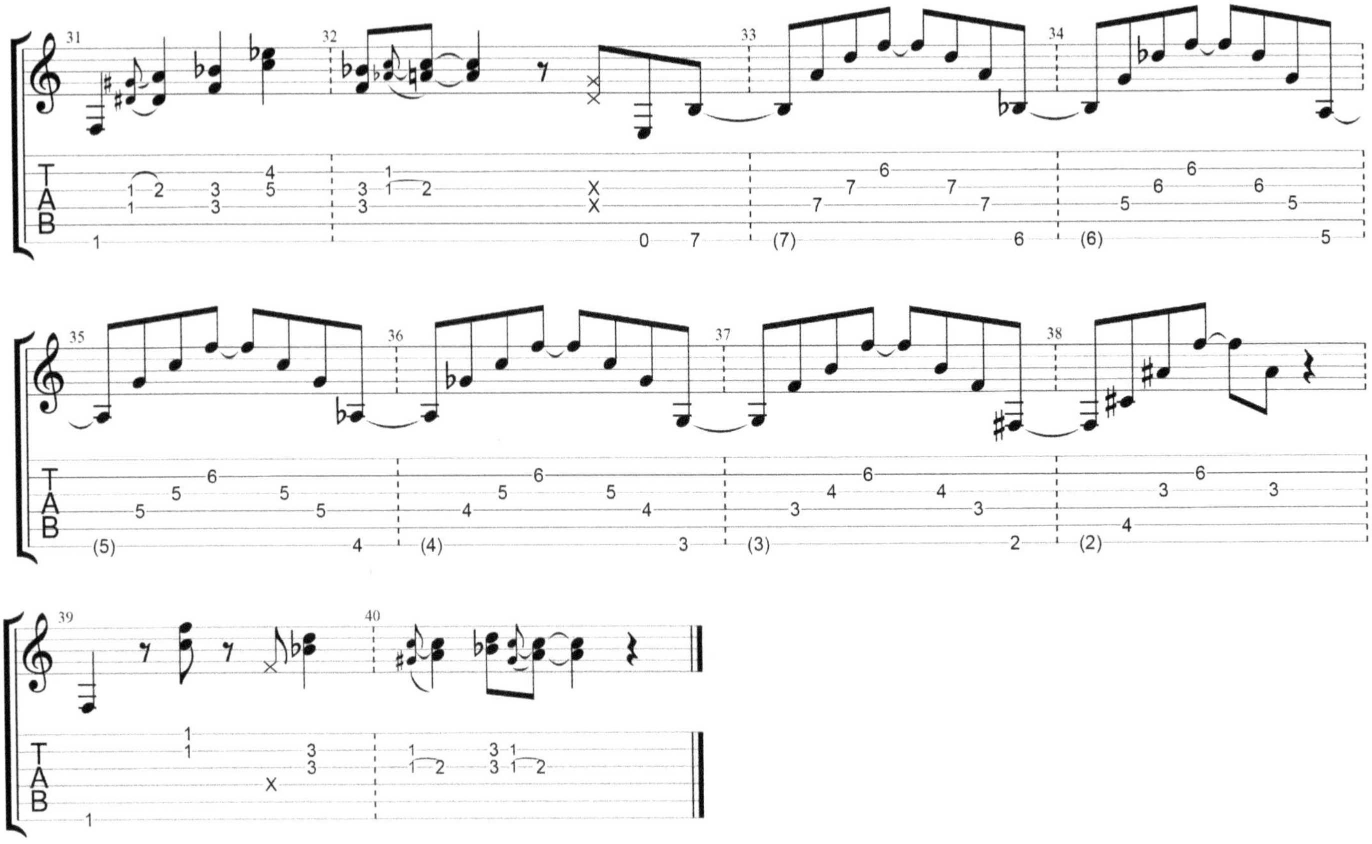

Chapter Six – Chromatic Licks and Enclosures

"Some people get very philosophical and cerebral about what they're trying to say with jazz. You don't need any prologues, you just play."

Another feature of Oscar's playing was his use of chromaticism and enclosures to build complex harmonic lines and motifs, which are both tried and tested bebop devices. They can be used to create beautiful lines that weave around the underlying harmony, sometimes sounding as if they will never resolve.

First we'll look at some licks using chromatic approach notes, then move on to enclosures. Finally, we'll look at some licks that blend the two approaches.

Technique tips

- A worthwhile exercise is to learn the main melodies to some of Charlie Parker's tunes (*Anthropology, Donna Lee,* and *Scrapple From the Apple* are particularly good examples). Parker's beautifully formed melodic lines are a masterclass in the use of chromaticism and you can learn a lot by isolating what he played over a particular chord.

First listen to Example 6a, then I'll explain the technique used to create it. This lick is played over the A section to the tune *Close Your Eyes* in the key of F minor.

Example 6a

Ideas like those in the above example can be created by adding chromatic passing notes to the arpeggio tones in each chord to build enhanced phrases. This style of jazz improvisation tends to be played with 1/8th note passages, and the musician will try to ensure that mostly chord tones, rather than passing notes, fall on the strong beats of the bar. This "outside-inside" sound is the heart of bebop.

To explain how the technique works, let's focus on the Fm7 chord in the *Close Your Eyes* progression. Look at the two Fm7 arpeggio diagrams below. The diagram on the left shows only the notes of an Fm7 arpeggio in 8th position. The diagram on the right shows every possible chromatic note you could play, located around the arpeggio notes, without moving away from 8th position.

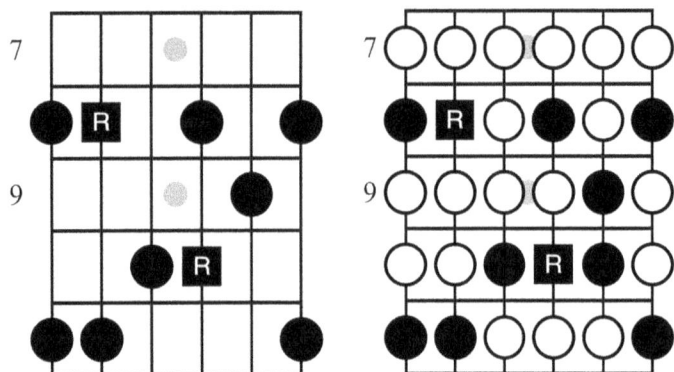

This diagram tells us that *any* combination of chord tones and passing notes can be used to create a lick. The only caveat is that it must sound good to our ears! Here's the kind of line that can be constructed using this idea (there's no audio for this exercise).

The line above begins with four arpeggio notes played in sequence, then chromatic notes are used to approach the arpeggio tones for the rest of the line. Instantly, it sounds like bebop. This is the principle used in the licks that follow.

Here are three Oscar-style lines, each of which contains runs that include chromatic notes, created using this technique.

Example 6b

Example 6c

Example 6d

Enclosures

Next we move onto the concept of *enclosures*. In simple terms, an enclosure surrounds a target note with notes either side (usually on the same string). This approach differs from chromaticism in that enclosures use a combination of scale tones and chromatic notes to surround the target. Let's illustrate this with a Cmaj7.

A typical enclosure lick would take the chord tones of the Cmaj7 chord and enclose them with a *scale note* above each chord tone, and either a scale note or chromatic note below. Play through the following example where the chord tones fall in the middle of each triplet.

Now play through this example based on a Dm7 chord shape played in 5th position. In this instance, a note located above each chord tone is played, then the chord tone itself, then a note below, then the chord tone again. Joe Pass often played this type of line.

There are many different variations that can be played once you understand the principle. This lick shows how enclosures can be used to create melodic phrases as part of a solo.

Example 6e

The remaining ideas in this chapter blend these two approaches. Parts of the line will be built on enclosures, spelling out an arpeggio, and other parts will be constructed from chromatic runs. Combining these ideas will create a contrast in your playing – a mix of dense chromatic runs and more intervallic-sounding enclosures. Work through the following seven examples and see if you can identify the enclosures and approach note ideas they include.

Example 6f

Example 6g

Example 6h

Example 6i

Example 6j

Example 6k

Example 6l

Chapter Seven – Fast Runs

"I knew someone would have to be a driving force within the group and I decided that would be me."

Oscar once said, "I'm an admirer of the beautiful long line which starts out and then reaches a point of definition. If you reach a point of definition, it validates all the other aspects of the line … I'm an advocate of the long line, but it's got to *mean something*."

In his playing, Oscar would improvise lines that were both long *and* fast, yet they were full of well-conceived melodic content. He would often play 1/16th note lines, but sometimes 1/32nd notes too, which had a dramatic effect and, of course, highlighted his stunning technique.

Technique tips

- There are some challenging lines in this chapter's examples – you have been warned! To learn them successfully, practice the lines with a metronome at a *slow* tempo. Play through them lots of times to commit the shape of each line to muscle memory. Make sure you can play each one smoothly several times before you think about speeding up the metronome.

- When playing 1/8th note jazz lines, guitarists tend to add a subtle bouncing triplet feel to help make the lines swing. When playing fast, this approach won't work – the lines need to be played straight, with an even emphasis. This is the only method to achieve a fluid sound at high speed.

If you're going to include a fast run in your solo, it can be dramatic to contrast it against something very simple. This might be an extreme example (I am a bit extreme!), but Example 7a begins with a simple bluesy "question" style lick. In bar three this is answered with a blistering 1/32nd note run that is quite unexpected.

A bluesy phrase occurs again in bar five which is answered with a slightly less dramatic swinging 1/16th note run. In bars 8-9 I deliberately begin to put the brakes on and play behind the beat. Take your time with bars 3-4 to nail the shape of the super-fast run.

Example 7a

Here's another example of how Oscar might sandwich a fast burst of notes in the middle of some slower phrases for dramatic effect. Example 7b begins with a deceptively lazy, bluesy phrase. In bar three this is contrasted with a 1/16th note run that crosses the bar line into bar four. Bar five has another blues lick, which is again followed by a long, fast run.

Example 7b

Next, try this example of playing 1/16th note phrases over a mid-tempo swing tune. Here I play 1/16th note lines over the A section of *Satin Doll* in the key of Bb Major. The lick begins with a cascading line that descends through the Cm7 and F7 chords with chromatic passing notes.

You'll notice lots of passing notes in these fast lines as it would be very difficult to play long 1/16th note phrases with just chord tones. I've gone to town with the long line for effect and I don't really pause for breath until bar ten. It's OK to do this once in a while but you don't want to overuse this idea!

Example 7c

Cm7 F7 Cm7 F7

OK, brace yourself – here are some very fast lines for you to work on! Imagine you are at the peak of a solo and you're going to play a stream of notes over the changes for a while, before bringing it all back down to earth. Here are two examples of how to play fast lines over the changes of *Sweet Georgia Brown*, played up tempo.

Example 7d

F7

Bb7

Eb7

Abmaj7   Bbm7   Eb7   Abmaj7   Gø7   C7b9

The next example in this frantic chapter is another pass of the changes of *Sweet Georgia Brown.* As fast as this is, played up to speed, you'll notice that even when I'm playing fast streams of notes, there are still occasional gaps in the lines. When you slow things right down, you'll see there are identifiable phrases. There are some long lines here, but there are still a few breaths inbetween the lines!

Example 7e

Let's bring things back down to earth with a more sedate bluesy idea over the C Major turnaround from examples 7a and 7b.

Example 7f

Remember, when working on fast licks, always start slow and focus on playing cleanly. Only increase your speed gradually, and in small increments. This will help you to lock the shape of the line into muscle memory.

Good luck working on your speed chops!

Chapter Eight – Modal Licks

"It doesn't matter what the instrument is, it's simply another means of expression. ... it still depends on you, and what you say that makes it valid or invalid."

One of the projects Oscar worked on in the 1970s was a collection of original compositions he referred to as the Africa Suite. He didn't perform many tunes from these compositions live, but one tune that regularly featured on our set list was *Nigerian Marketplace*.

Unusually for Oscar, the A section is more modal in its approach. Beginning with an Am9 chord, the progression descends a whole tone to Gm9. It then shifts down another tone to Fm9, and is followed by an E9#11 then a resolution to Ebmaj9#11. After a more complex middle sixteen bars, the tune returns to the modal sequence.

At the beginning of the 1950s, articulating the chord changes in your solo was so much a part of jazz that often, at recording sessions, the musicians would only be given a chord chart – no melody. By the end of the 50's, however, jazz musicians were restless to explore new territory and many began composing modal tunes. Modal tunes were often sparse on chord changes, because the music was more about experimenting with different scale-based lines over static chords. Miles Davis' *So What* and John Coltrane's *Impressions* are classic early examples where the entire tune is founded on one chord that shifts up and down by a semitone. Wayne Shorter's *Footprints* is another example, composed using chords from the harmonized Dorian mode.

The challenge for jazz guitarists is to create interesting melodic phrases over several bars of a static chord. In *Nigerian Marketplace* we have static chords *and* shifting tonal centers: A minor to G minor, leading to Eb Major.

Note: when the sequence changes to Fm9, this is a disguised ii V I in the key of Eb Major. Normally, the sequence would read Fm9 – Bb7 – Ebmaj7. In *Nigerian Marketplace*, the Eb9#11 chord is a b5 substitution for Bb7, and the Ebmaj7 has been extended and altered to an Ebmaj9#11.

The first group of example licks deal with the most obvious modal shift in this tune: A minor to G minor. In modal jazz, it's normal to treat each chord as a tonal center in its own right, so here we are mostly concerned with creating colors and textures over the chords in isolation.

In Example 8a I'm thinking in terms of the relative major key for each of the tonal centers. C Major is the relative major key of A minor, and Bb Major is the relative key of G minor. This line doubles back on itself to create a cascading effect.

Example 8a

The melody played over the Am9 chord in Example 8b is based around the common Cmaj7 chord shape played in seventh position. The top note of the Cmaj7 voicing (a B note on the high E string, 7th fret) is the 9th of an Am9 chord. This idea is transposed down a tone for the Gm9 chord, so now we're using a Bbmaj7 chord shape. In bars 9-16, the whole idea is played again an octave higher, which is an easy way to make your licks go further.

Example 8b

Next, here's a challenging little lick which creates a fast, effective sextuplet looping sequence in C Major.

Treat each six-note phrase as two separate fretting hand movements. First, execute the three notes on the high E string with a hammer-on/pull-off using the index and middle finger. Then, play the three notes on the B string with a hammer-on/pull-off using the ring and index fingers. Your fretting hand will need to jump back a bit to accommodate the second hammer-on/pull-off, then forward again for the next loop. Take things ultra-slow until the transition sounds really smooth.

Example 8c

Here's an idea that uses the basic blues scale over each chord, but keeps things interesting by sequencing the notes.

Example 8d

The next lick uses the upper notes of each chord's minor 9 arpeggio. It's a four-note phrase and the interest is created by breaking up the rhythms.

Example 8e

The next group of licks focuses on the remaining part of the A section harmony – the "disguised" ii V I in Eb Major. The b5 substitution in bar two (Eb9#11 in place of Bb7) creates a nice dissonance and gives us scope to play some spicer lines. This section is, of course, based on more traditional jazz harmony.

In the first example, bar two is the main point of interest and there are two jazz substitution ideas at work:

The first is the common idea of superimposing minor tonalities over dominant chords. When you encounter a dominant chord, you can substitute a minor chord whose root is a perfect fifth above it. So, over our E dominant chord we can play B minor ideas because B is a perfect fifth above E.

We've already encountered the second idea: to move melodic/harmonic ideas in minor thirds. The phrase that begins on the final note of bar one and continues into bar two, spells an Abm9 chord shape. This is just the Bm9 shape played a minor third lower. I could equally have shifted the Bm9 up a minor third to Dm9. Or played all three. Try hitting your open low E string, then play the upper notes of Abm9 – Bm9 – Dm9 – Bm9, with the low E ringing throughout. This is a common sound in modern jazz.

Example 8f

Example 8g uses a similar superimposition idea. Over the Fm9 chord in bar one, I play a simple phrase using notes from an Abmaj7 chord (Ab Major is the relative major key of F minor). I continue this idea in bar two, where the first seven notes of the phrase are from an Abmaj7 arpeggio.

Next, the focus shifts to the underlying E9#11 chord where the second triplet "trill" (B string, frets 11 and 12) highlights the #11 note.

Example 8g

The following example begins with an Abmaj7 arpeggio lick over the Fm9. The line that spans the end of bar one/beginning of bar two begins with an augmented shape that eventually leads to the #11 note (an A# note played on the B string, 11th fret). Thereafter, the rest of the lick is a bluesy line containing lots of approach notes.

Example 8h

In bar two of Example 8i, E minor triad inversions are played over the E9#11 chord (D B G – B G D – G D B).

You might wonder how an E minor sound works over an altered dominant chord, but the note B is the 5th of E9#11, and the D is the b7. It's only the G note that is dissonant (it should be a G# – the 3rd), but this just gives the line an outside/inside sound, as the G is only played fleetingly.

Example 8i

In this final example, an Abmaj7 arpeggio is superimposed over Fm9 in bar one. In bar two the E minor triad over E9#11 is used again, but this time the notes are sequenced. In the final bar, the sound of Ebmaj9#11 is spelled out with an arpeggio and I add in the 6th of the chord (a C note). This means that for much of this long phrase I'm playing the notes F, A and C, which are the notes of an F major triad.

Ebmaj9#11 is a complex chord to think about, so it might help you to know this trick of playing the notes of a major triad *a tone above* the root. The major triad notes F, A and C, form the 9th, #11 and 6th of Ebmaj9#11.

Example 8j

Chapter Nine – Performance Piece: OP's Blues x 2

The final two chapters of this book contain three full solos that bring together as many of the Oscar-inspired ideas as possible that we've explored in this book. I suggest working through the solos in four-bar chunks to get the licks under your fingers.

In this chapter there are two choruses of the blues for you to tackle. This first example contains mainly single-note lines. You'll hear Oscar's characteristic bluesy phrasing, some double-stops, and also some question and answer phrases.

Example 9a

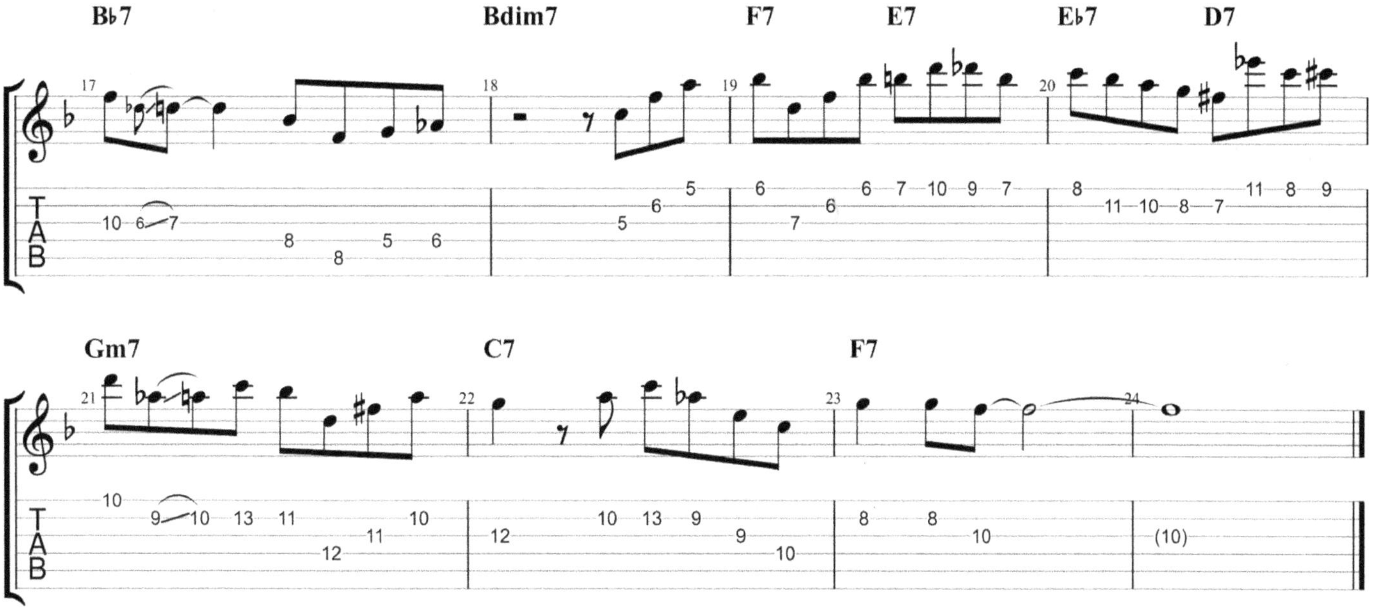
B♭7
Bdim7
F7
E7
E♭7
D7
Gm7
C7
F7

The second chorus of this blues in F features more octave ideas and some block chord passages. In bars 17-20, look out for the lazily phrased pedal tone idea that purposely drags behind the beat to mimic the slurred lines that Oscar would play.

Example 9b

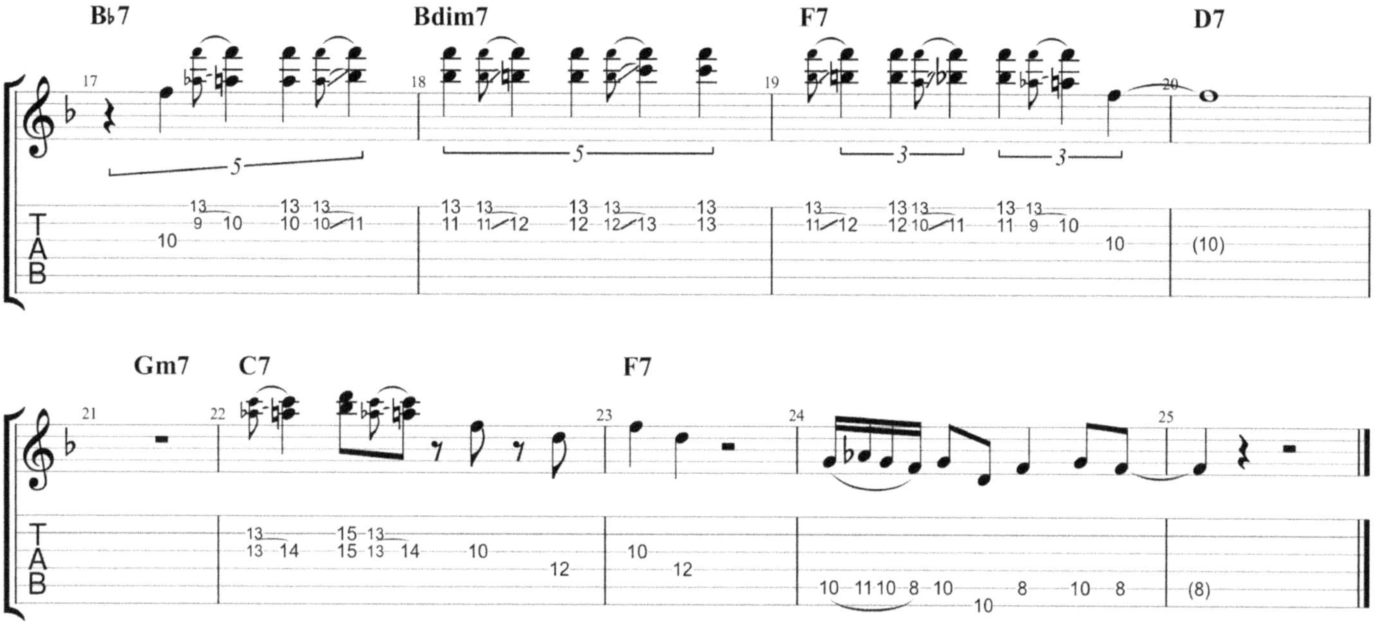
B♭7
Bdim7
F7
D7
Gm7
C7
F7
TAB

Chapter Ten – Performance Piece: Falling In Love With Love

This final piece is based on the chords to the song *Falling in Love With Love* (with a few chord substitutions added). It's a tune that Oscar loved to play, and comes from the musical *The Boys From Syracuse* by Rodgers and Hart. You can hear a lovely version by Oscar on the album *The Oscar Peterson Trio at Zardi's*, which features the legendary musicians Ray Brown and Herb Ellis.

This performance features lots of Oscar-style enclosure licks that are played with a bluesy inflection. Once again, break this piece down into smaller sections to work on the more challenging passages.

Example 10a

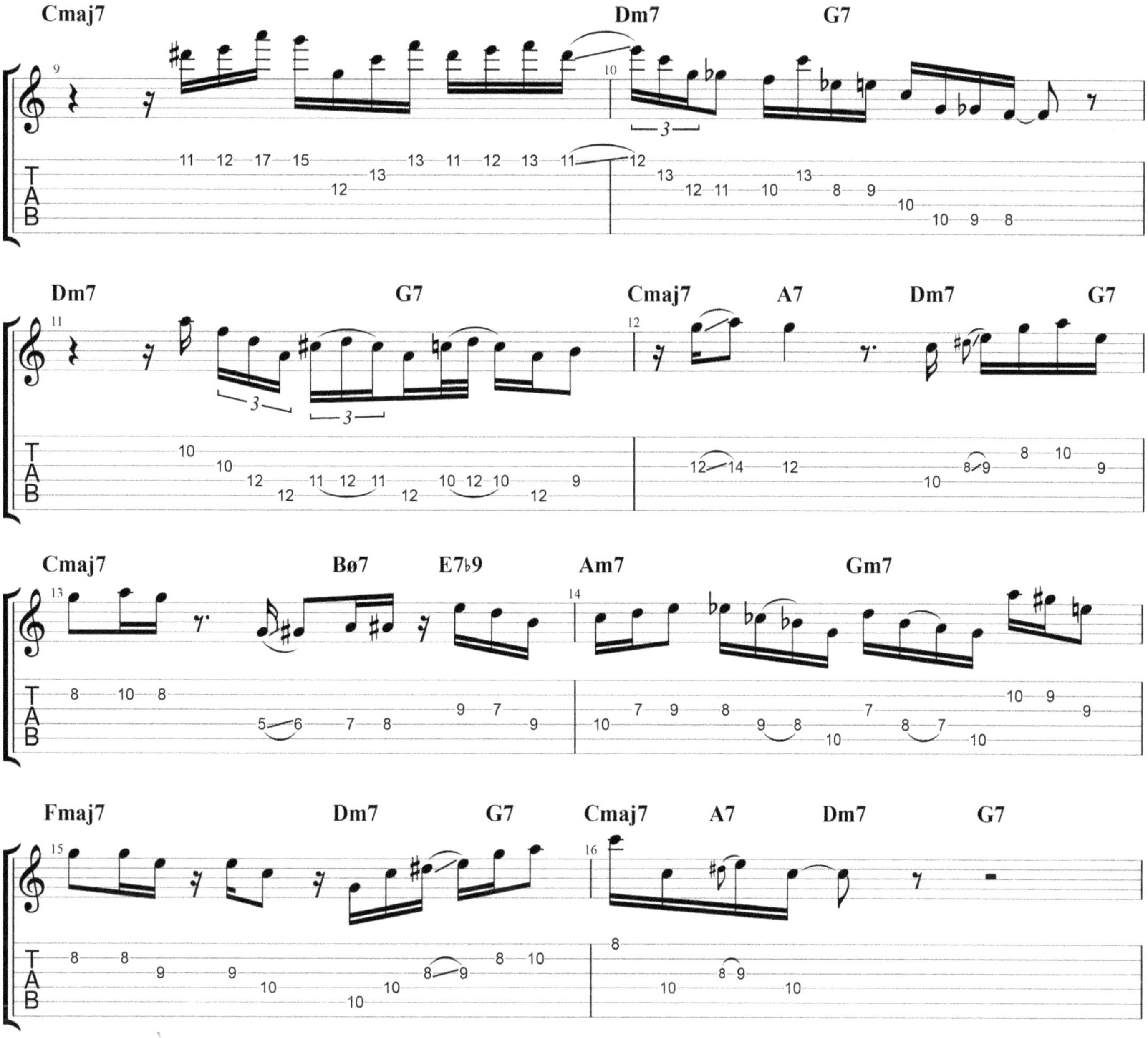
Cmaj7 Dm7 G7
Dm7 G7 Cmaj7 A7 Dm7 G7
Cmaj7 Bø7 E7♭9 Am7 Gm7
Fmaj7 Dm7 G7 Cmaj7 A7 Dm7 G7

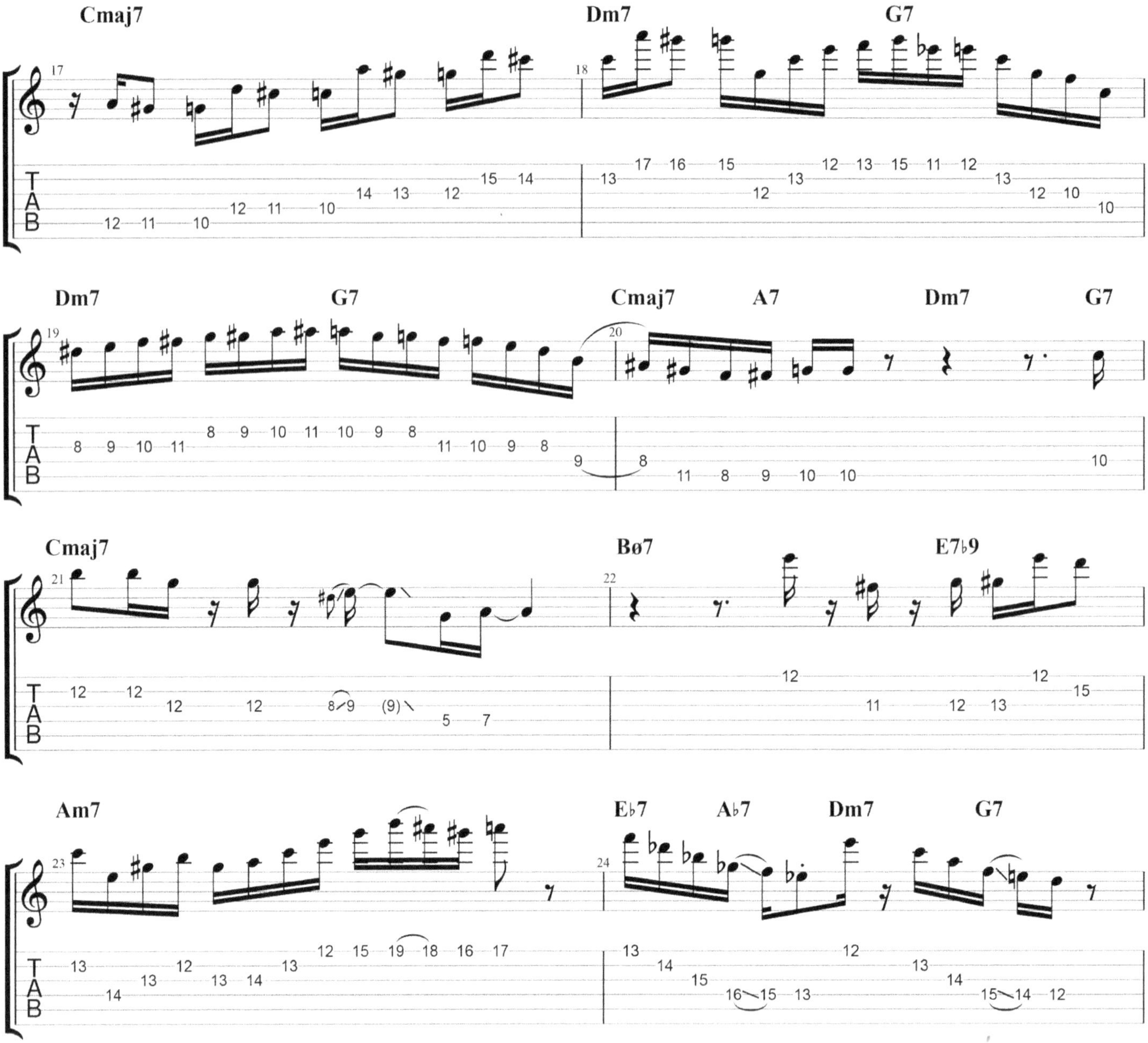
Cmaj7
Dm7
G7
Dm7
G7
Cmaj7
A7
Dm7
G7
Cmaj7
Bø7
E7♭9
Am7
E♭7
A♭7
Dm7
G7

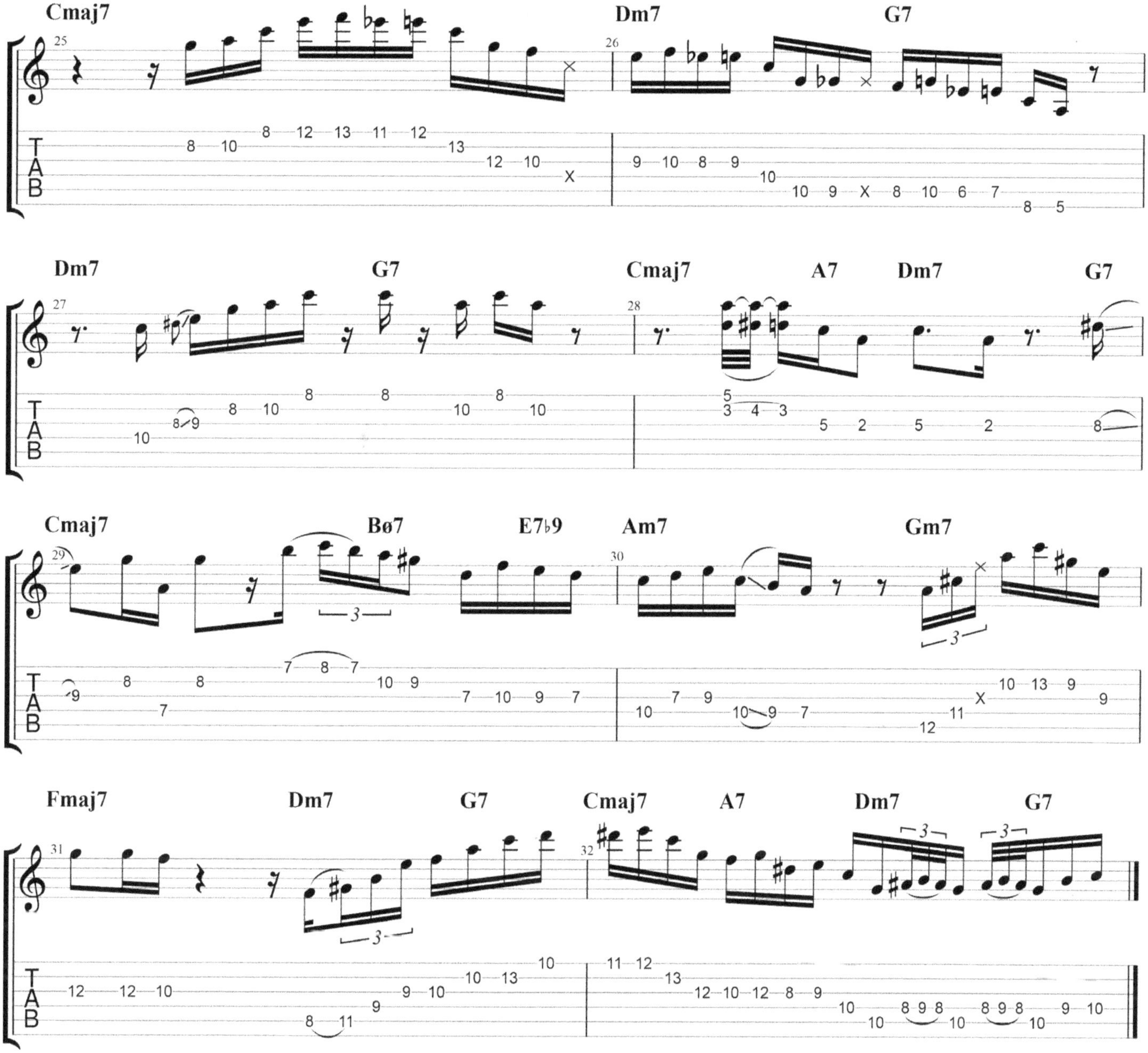
Cmaj7
Dm7
G7
Dm7
G7
Cmaj7
A7
Dm7
G7
Cmaj7
Bø7
E7♭9
Am7
Gm7
Fmaj7
Dm7
G7
Cmaj7
A7
Dm7
G7

Conclusion

I hope you've enjoyed this journey through the jazz concepts of Oscar Peterson. Oscar loved to play with guitar players and his bands featured some of the all-time greats: Barney Kessel, Herb Ellis, Irving Ashby (Nat King Cole's guitar player) and Joe Pass. I still have to pinch myself when I think that I got to be his guitar player too.

Oscar was the consummate musician. Joe Pass commented that the only musicians he knew who had come close to total mastery of their instrument were Oscar Peterson and Art Tatum. Oscar's knowledge of jazz techniques was both broad and deep, and there is still much to learn from listening to his music. We all love jazz guitar, but I hope this book has inspired you to investigate how other instruments can inform our playing.

Keeping learning and listening,

Ulf.

More Jazz Guitar Books From Fundamental Changes

100 Classic Jazz Licks For Guitar

Advanced Jazz Guitar Concepts

Beginner Gypsy Jazz Guitar

Fundamental Changes in Jazz Guitar

Jazz Bebop Blues Guitar

Jazz Blues Soloing for Guitar

Jazz Guitar Chord Creativity

Jazz Guitar Chord Mastery

Jazz Guitar Chord Tone Soloing

Martin Taylor – Walking Bass for Jazz Guitar

Martin Taylor Beyond Chord Melody

Martin Taylor Single Note Soloing for Jazz Guitar

Martin Taylor's Jazz Guitar Licks Phrase Book

Minor ii V Mastery for Jazz Guitar

Modern Jazz Guitar Concepts

Rhythm Changes for Jazz Guitar

The First 100 Jazz Chords for Guitar

Voice Leading Jazz Guitar